W9-ABE-768

THE TIME TRAVELER'S GUIDE

EGYPTIAN TOWN

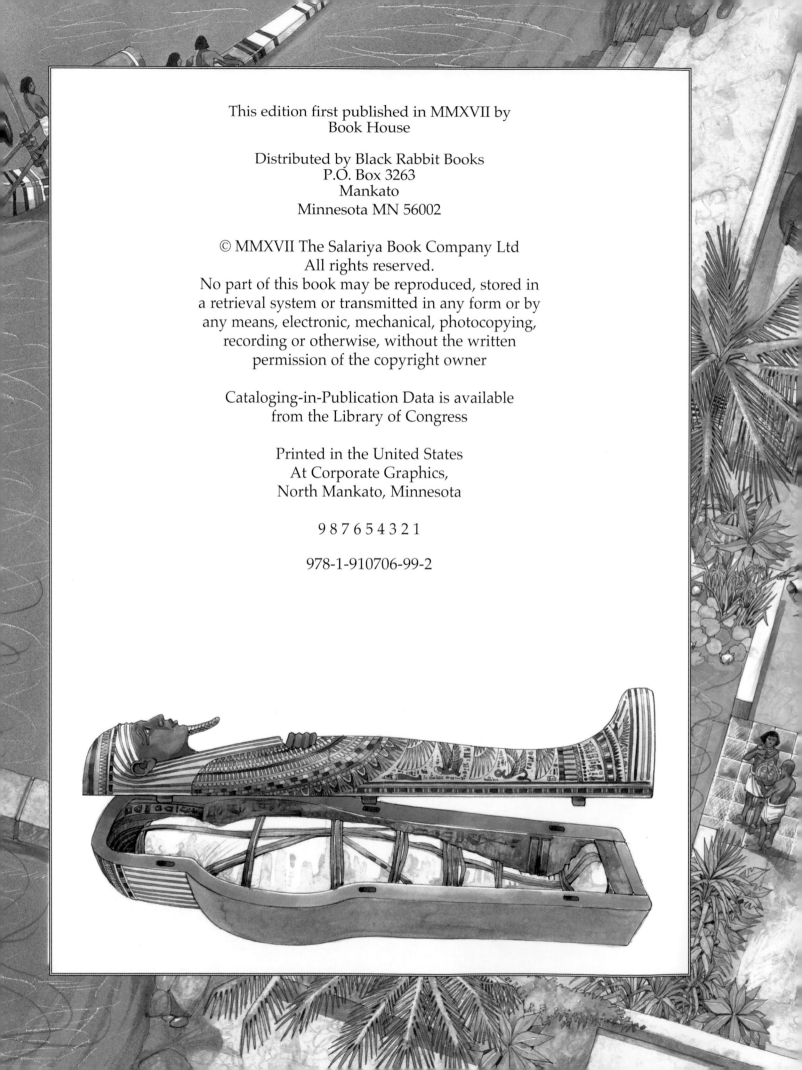

This edition first published in MMXVII by
Book House

Distributed by Black Rabbit Books
P.O. Box 3263
Mankato
Minnesota MN 56002

Cataloging-in-Publication Data is available
from the Library of Congress

Printed in the United States
At Corporate Graphics,
North Mankato, Minnesota

9 8 7 6 5 4 3 2 1

978-1-910706-99-2

THE TIME TRAVELER'S GUIDE

EGYPTIAN TOWN

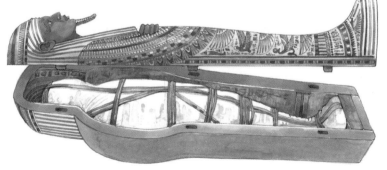

Written by Scott Steedman
Illustrated by David Antram

BOOK HOUSE

CONTENTS

INTRODUCTION

Over 5,000 years ago, the Egyptians created the world's first great civilization by the River Nile. For the next twenty-five centuries it was the richest and most powerful civilization in the world.

This book is about a New Kingdom town in around 1200 BCE. It is not a capital, just an everyday city. Its wealth can be seen in the pharaoh's palace and the great temple. It has poor districts where servants and craftsmen live in cramped conditions. Merchants and government officials arrive by boat and hurry through the narrow streets. And in the fields by the river, farmers work the soil just as their families have done for centuries.

AROUND THE TOWN

Workers' Houses
Ordinary workers live in tiny mud-brick apartments, built one upon the other. They share the small smoky rooms with children, grandparents, cats, and even pet monkeys.

Mummification
Dead Egyptians are turned into mummies in the embalming tents. This sacred work is performed by priests from the nearby temple. Find out more on pages 22–23.

Farms and Fields
The green fields by the river are ideal for growing wheat, barley, and flax. The farmers, whose homes are simple mud-brick houses, also rear cattle and geese and tend their vegetable gardens. See pages 14–15.

River Traffic
People, messages, and goods all travel by river. Boats, powered either by oars or sails, bring travelers, fishermen, or merchants from faraway lands. On pages 12–13, the men are hunting a hippopotamus.

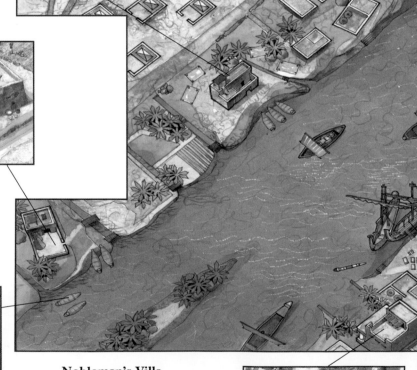

Nobleman's Villa
Some members of the royal family live in the palace. Others have villas in quiet locations, with shady gardens and well-stocked fish ponds. Find out more on pages 34–35.

Valley of the Kings
For centuries, Egypt's greatest pharaohs have been buried in this desolate spot. It is guarded day and night, and visits are strictly forbidden. Visit pages 18–19.

Mortuary Temple
To pay respects to a dead king or relative, Egyptians visit the mortuary temple on pages 24–25. They recite prayers and leave offerings of food and wine.

Pharoah's Palace
This is just one of the pharaoh's many houses. When he visits the town, he stays here with his many wives and servants. Princes, princesses, and officials live here all year round. See more on pages 20–21.

Temple
The biggest and most impressive building in the town is the temple, home to priests, scribes (professional writers), and officials. It includes craft workshops, storehouses, and kitchens. See pages 26–27.

Market
There are very few stores, and most goods are bought and sold in the crowded market, close to the pier. The marketplace is on pages 30–31.

Harbor
All day long, goods such as wheat, wine, building stone, horses, and dried fish are loaded and unloaded in the bustling harbor. You can see more on pages 28–29.

Merchants' Houses
Rich merchants live in luxurious town houses near the quay. These have large rooms for the family, and smaller ones for the servants. See pages 32–33.

FISHING IN THE RIVER

The marshes by the River Nile teem with fish and ducks, long-legged cranes, and other birds. Rich Egyptians love fishing and hunting birds. These exciting sports are ways of proving their skill and courage. Ordinary people fish and hunt, too, but to provide food for their families rather than for sport.

Fishing and hunting also have a religious meaning for Egyptians. The hippopotamus, for instance, is a dangerous animal that kills hundreds of people every year. In Egyptian legend it is a symbol of the evil god, Seth. Hunters in flimsy rafts risk their lives spearing hippopotamuses. By killing one, they score a victory for good, and help to restore order to the world.

THE FARMING YEAR

Most ancient Egyptians are farmers whose lives follow the rhythms of the River Nile. It does not rain very often in Egypt and it is hot all year round. But in late spring every year the Nile floods its banks and brings water to the fields. This is **Akhet**, the time of flood. Farmers rest during this season.

It is followed by **Peret**, when the waters fall, leaving fertile black soil on the fields. This is the time to plow the fields, sow crops, and build new irrigation channels.

Next comes **Shemu**, the time of harvest, when everybody works hard to bring in the crops before the Nile rises again.

CRAFTWORKERS

Next to the town's temple is a large workshop complex where skilled craftworkers produce beautiful goods.

Sculptors carve statues, potters sweat over their wheels, and jewelers make items from gold inlaid with gemstones. Carpenters make furniture, chariots, and mummy cases, while glassmakers shape bowls and jars in vivid colors. Elsewhere, painters, metalworkers, and weavers are busy.

Workers put in four hours of work each morning. Then they have lunch and a nap before working another four-hour shift in the afternoon. The "working week" is ten days, followed by a rest day.

PYRAMIDS AND TOMBS

The Egyptians build their tombs on the west bank of the Nile. This is the Land of the Dead, where the Sun god Amun-Ra sets over the desert every evening. The Sun's journey inspires the Egyptians. After death, they believe that a person's spirit travels through the underworld, like the Sun at night. If it survives the dangerous journey, the spirit rises again, like the sun in the morning.

To prepare for the next world, rich Egyptians are buried with clothing, furniture, games, loaves of bread, and fine wines. Their tombs are cut deep into the rock. The walls are painted with magic spells and pictures of the gods, to help them on their way.

THE PHARAOH'S PALACE

The pharaoh lives in a palace by the Nile. The Egyptians believe he is the son of the Sun god Amun-Ra, sent to Earth to protect Egypt and its people. His power is awesome. He judges criminals and leads the army in battle. Everyone in the palace spends their time pleasing this living god.

The pharoah has hundreds of servants to look after him. On holidays, they carry him through streets of cheering people. Musicians and dancing girls perform for him, and wrestlers fight to entertain him.

PREPARING A MUMMY

To live forever, an Egyptian must preserve his or her body for the next world. This process is called mummification. It is carried out on the Nile's east bank by priests called embalmers, and takes 80 days. The priests bless every stage of the process, chanting spells and sprinkling the dead body with sacred water.

Early in Egypt's history, only kings and queens were mummified. But now everyone who can afford it has their body preserved. You can buy all the accessories in a range of styles to suit your tastes and budget.

A MORTUARY TEMPLE

The pharaoh, Egypt's beloved god-king, has died. His body has been mummified, and now it is time for him to travel across the Nile to the Land of the Dead, where he will rejoin the gods.

The day of the funeral is a national holiday, and people come from far away. Huge crowds watch as priests steer the pharaoh's body across the Nile and carry it to the mortuary temple. Here, priests perform the last rites and bury the king in a secret tomb.

For years to come, the temple priests will make offerings of food to the spirit of the dead pharaoh who is now a god.

AT THE TEMPLE

The town's temple is dedicated to one of Egypt's many gods. The Egyptians see it as the god's house. Only priests are allowed to enter the sacred inner rooms. At the heart of the complex stands a golden shrine containing a statue of the god.

Every morning, as the first rays of sunlight enter the room, the priests open the shrine. Burning incense and reciting prayers, they dress the statue and place a meal before it. This process is repeated several times a day. The temple has its own workshops, kitchens, and farms where the food for offerings is produced.

THE QUAYSIDE

Trade and transport center on the Nile. Egypt has few roads because they are hard to build on the desert. The great river is the country's only highway, linking every important town, temple, and tomb.

When a pharaoh visits a town, he arrives in his spectacular royal barge. Merchants sail up and down the river, taking goods from one place to another and supplying whatever is needed. Trading ships, pleasure boats, and fishermen's rafts jostle for a place at the quayside. All day long, cargo such as dried fish, wine, wheat, horses, and building stone are loaded and unloaded.

THE MARKETPLACE

On market days, the people of the town head for the large marketplace by the quayside. Farmers come by boat to sell their produce. Families stock up with wheat or barley to bake bread and brew beer, and buy linen to make clothes. Wine growers haggle over the price of their wine, sold in amphorae (tall clay pots). Pet cats, honey, and luxuries such as walnuts, plums, and watermelons are all on sale.

Foreign traders attract crowds. The Nubians sell ebony and ivory from the south. The Palestinians have horses, silver, and fine cedar wood to sell.

A MERCHANT'S HOUSE

A rich merchant has a house in the center of town, close to the quayside, the temple, and the palace. He may also have a country villa, where he can hunt or relax in the hot summer months.

His town house, built of mud bricks like most Egyptian buildings, has three main floors. The ground floor is the servants' quarters. On the first floor are the reception rooms and family bedrooms. These have high ceilings, brightly painted with plant and animal designs. Upstairs is an office, guest rooms, and store rooms. The roof is used for cooking. It is also the coolest place to relax on a hot evening.

33

A NOBLEMAN'S FEAST

A member of the royal family has invited all his friends to a feast. As the host and hostess greet their guests, servants hand them garlands of flowers to put around their necks, and perfumed wax cones to place on their heads.

Most of the guests sit on cushions at small tables and servants bring them wine and rich food. The host and important guests sit on elegant wooden chairs. Musicians play during the meal.

After the plates have been cleared away, dancing girls perform acrobatic routines. The wine flows endlessly. Any guest who drinks too much can ask a servant to bring them a bowl so they can be sick.

TIME-TRAVELER'S GUIDE

GETTING AROUND

The best way to get to any Egyptian town is by boat. Ferries come and go all the time, so just go down to the harbor and ask about the next sailing. The captain will tell you the cost. Prices vary with demand and season—they are highest during the flood, when the river is treacherous—so be prepared to bargain just before the ship sails. Your fellow passengers may include cattle, horses, or pet baboons!

If you are heading for Libya or the Faiyum Oasis, you can hitch a ride across the desert with a merchant's caravan. You can hire a donkey, or better still a horse (camels have not yet been introduced to Egypt). Make sure to stock up with water before you leave—the desert is a harsh place, and water will cost a lot more in any oasis along your route.

In town, most people get around on foot—except the pharaoh, who is carried everywhere in his golden litter.

WHAT TO WEAR

Egypt is very hot all year round. In the daytime, the temperature is

almost always over 86°F (30°C), so dress lightly. Don't be shocked by the nakedness you will see everywhere. The locals are not shy about their bodies—farmers and manual workers wear very few clothes. In town, people dress up more, but no one wears underclothes, so you can often see their bodies through the thin fabrics.

Most clothes are made of white linen, the thinner the better. Men usually wear simple wraparound skirts and leave their chests bare, or throw a light cloak over their shoulders. Women wear long, clinging dresses. On formal occasions, both men and women wear longer, more elaborate outfits and lots of cosmetics, especially the thick black eye paint called kohl. If you are invited to an important dinner, ask your host's servants to press hundreds of tiny pleats into your outfit. And a wig of human hair is a must for formal occasions.

Poor people go barefoot, but you should buy some sandals. They will protect you from scorpions and snakes as well as sharp rocks. You can buy a pair of reed sandals from a stand on the edge of the marshes. If you have enough money, buy a leather pair from the saddler in the market. They will last longer.

At night, it can get very cold, especially out in the desert. So always carry a linen cape or a woolen shawl with you.

PERSONAL HYGIENE

Egyptians are very clean and tidy, so you must wash well or you will give offense. There are no bathtubs. Instead, the servants will bring you a jug of water and a bowl so you can wash your body every morning. You must clean your hands and face before and after every meal. Wealthy people get their servants to pour water over them, sometimes through a sieve to make a shower.

You should also ask for a little salt to rinse out your mouth in the morning. This ritual is known as sen shem shem, which means "cleansing of mouth and teeth."

To stop their skin drying out in the hot climate, Egyptians rub themselves with greasy ointments made from cat, hippopotamus, or crocodile fat. Women also wear deodorants that smell of dates or frankincense, or exotic oils such as myrrh.

Even children wear kohl, an eye makeup produced from black minerals. It keeps away flies, acts as a disinfectant, and protects the eyes from bright sunlight. Women also color their nails, palms, and the soles of their feet with a yellow dye made from the leaves of the henna plant.

ACCIDENTS

Wild animals are a cause for concern. The most dangerous are hippopotamuses and crocodiles, which are everywhere in the

TIME-TRAVELER'S GUIDE

river. But snakes are also common and they kill even more people each year. The asp, or Egyptian cobra, is the most dangerous. Scorpions also cause many deaths.

The Egyptians protect their families from beasts by making offerings to the gods or setting up altars in their houses. If you want to do this too, go to the temple and ask a priest to explain how to do it. You will have to make a small donation to the temple.

WRITING

For foreigners, Egyptian hieroglyphs (picture writing) are both fascinating and confusing. There are more than 700 different symbols. You will see hieroglyphic inscriptions on statues, monuments, jewelry, and good luck charms everywhere you go. Here are a few clues to help you decipher them.

Every word is written exactly as it sounds, using symbols to represent sounds or whole words. A few symbols are simple pictures, easy to work out—for instance a sun, pronounced "ra," means "day." But most pictures are more abstract, and have different meanings according to the way they are used. Learning the 24 letters of the alphabet is a good start, but you should also look out for other clues to help you understand a text. For example, a crouching man means the subject is a person, while a pair of legs means "walking" or "running."

Also pay attention to the way animals or people are facing. If they have been drawn looking to the right, the text is read from left to right; if they face left, it is read the other way. The same text can also be written in columns read from the top or the bottom.

Another thing to look for are cartouches, ovals which contain the name of a pharaoh. Learn to recognize

TIME-TRAVELER'S GUIDE

the cartouche of the present pharaoh, plus a few famous names such as Thutmose III and Ramses the Great, then you will be able to date statues, buildings, obelisks, and so on from their inscriptions.

Don't worry if you really can't make sense of hieroglyphs—most Egyptians cannot read or write either. The only ones who can do so with ease are the scribes, but they spent four or five years at a special school learning how to master the language. For them, learning to read and write was a way to have a good career. For letters, official documents, marriage contracts, and stories, they use another script called hieratic. This is a simplified version of hieroglyphs and is

always read from right to left.

PAPERWORK

Egypt is a very bureaucratic country, and sometimes it seems as if you need a papyrus (the local type of paper made from reeds) to do anything. If you are caught without the right documents, you will have to visit the House of Life ("per ankh" in Egyptian), a part of the temple complex. The scribes who work here will draw up any document you need, for a fee. For simple requests, such as a Book of the Dead or a wedding contract, they use

standard papyruses, simply adding your name in hieroglyphs in the right places. They will write out more complicated documents, such as official letters, specially for you, but this service will cost you more.

Many Houses of Life are attached to a library, the House of Books. You will find all the classics of Egyptian science, religion, and literature there, on papyrus rolls crammed into hollows in the walls. But you will have to befriend a priest to get in: these treasures are very closely guarded.

FOOD AND DRINK

You will soon get used to bread and onions, served at lunch and dinner throughout Egypt.

TIME-TRAVELER'S GUIDE

Most meals are also accompanied by vegetables such as beans, lentils, chick peas, green peas, leeks, olives, radishes, cucumbers, and a type of lettuce. Aniseed, cumin, dill, fennel, marjoram, mustard, thyme, and cilantro are all used to add flavor to meals, but pepper is unknown. Dessert is usually fruit, such as figs, palm fruits, pomegranates, dates, plums, or watermelons, or sweet pastries.

Egypt is a paradise for vegetarians. Even fish and duck, the most common meats, are not eaten every day. Red meat is rare, and probably beyond your budget. Poor Egyptians only taste it on feast days or at ceremonies such as weddings, when the family will slaughter a cow or pig. If you are lucky enough to be invited to a banquet, you may taste the best meat of all, game from the hunt. Antelope, gazelle, wild boar, ostrich, or Barbary sheep may all be on the menu. You could also be offered fish roe, ostrich eggs, or roast wild birds such as cranes, ducks, quails, and geese.

Egyptians drink beer with most meals. Be warned: it is home brewed, and can be thick with sediment, so use a straw. Wine is also common, though more expensive. The best vintages are made from grapes, but date and palm vines are also on the menu, and can be very good. The children can drink grape or date juice, which is often safer than water.

GOING OUT

Restaurants don't exist as we know them. But you will find food for sale from stalls on every corner. If you are invited to a meal with a poor family, expect to eat squatting around a big table. Use your hands or pieces of bread to scoop the food out of a shared bowl. At the end of the meal your host will pour water over your hands to wash them.

In the evening, you can get a drink

TIME-TRAVELER'S GUIDE

in one of the town's many beerhouses. These are excellent spots to meet locals, perhaps over a board game such as senet. Expect dancing, singing, and storytelling. Egyptians like enjoying themselves, and drunkenness is common. There is no set closing time for the beer-houses, and at festivals the beer will be served until late.

You will hear music everywhere, at food stalls, in beer houses, and at the market. Even in the fields, a boy will often play the flute while the workers are gathering in the harvest.

GIFTS AND SOUVENIRS

Jewelry and lucky charms are excellent gifts to take home for friends. You will find wonderful necklaces, bracelets, and rings in the market, many made of gold from the Eastern Desert. Egyptian jewelry often includes figures of gods or sacred animals, such as scarab beetles, and inscriptions of magic spells. You can also order rings or pendants with your name, or the name of a friend, inscribed in hieroglyphs in a cartouche.

Shabtis also make good gifts. These small, mummy-shaped figures are made of faience or wood. They are meant to be buried with a mummy, and contain a spell stating that they will work the fields for their owner in the afterlife. The Egyptians like to be buried with 365 of them, one for each day of the year.

You will find children's wooden toys carved to look like wild animals. Many have moveable parts, such as lions or hippopotamuses with teeth and big mouths that open and close. Also popular are clay models of animals and mummies.

TOILETS

Only the rich have proper toilets: two blocks of stone, separated by a gap with a bucket of sand. The best toilets have wooden seats. But don't be shy if you are caught out in the street. Most Egyptians relieve themselves out of

TIME-TRAVELER'S GUIDE

doors, in specially marked corners or by the river. Women and children collect human and animal dung, mix it with straw, and dry it on their roofs. In winter, they will burn it as fuel.

SPORTS

If you enjoy hunting, Egypt is a perfect holiday destination. The desert is home to many wild beasts which can be hunted with bow and arrow or spear from a chariot. Your guide will control the horses while you fire from a high platform at the back. The most popular game animals are gazelles, antelopes, wild bulls, ostriches, and wild sheep. You can go after lions, hyenas, or leopards, but that is dangerous and expensive.

The marshes are home to other game, including fish, crocodiles, and hippopotamuses. Wild birds are hunted from papyrus rafts, using throwing sticks like heavy boomerangs.

Swimming in the river is popular, especially during the yearly flood. The Egyptians also enjoy ball games, gymnastics, fencing with long sticks, and dancing. Girls always dance with girls and boys with boys.

When you arrive, check if any sports events are coming up. Archery contests and fencing, boxing, and wrestling matches often take place at the palace, to the cheers of a huge crowd, including the pharoah.

MONEY AND SHOPPING

Egypt has no official money, so most buying and selling is done by bartering: swapping different types of goods. Expert shoppers know what things are worth. Most sales are paid in common goods such as wheat and linen. To get a good deal, you should come to Egypt with some items that are rare and highly valued, such as wood, incense, or ivory.

Some goods are given a value in debens, equal to

TIME-TRAVELER'S GUIDE

a piece of copper weighing about 3.2 oz (90g). A goat is worth one deben, while a good wooden bed costs 2.5 debens.

FOR THE CHILDREN

Egyptians love children. They play and run wild in the streets, but there is always an adult keeping an eye on them.

One place where Egyptian children are well behaved is at scribe school. An old Egyptian proverb says: "A boy's ears are on his back: he hears when he is beaten."

WHEN TO VISIT

To avoid the heat, the best time to visit Egypt is the winter, from December to February. This corresponds with Peret, the seasons of sowing and plowing. Unless you are coming for the New Year festival, try to avoid traveling during Akhet, the time of flood. This is the hottest season, and the humidity can be unbearable. The high waters also make it difficult or even impossible to get about. In a year of high floods, many monuments are completely cut off.

Try to come for one of Egypt's festivals. The biggest is the New Year, a five-day holiday to mark the first sighting of Sirius, which the Egyptians call the "Dog Star." This is usually around July 19. Every town celebrates the feast day of its god, when priests carry the statue through the streets and there are masked dancers.

But the very best time to visit is during the sed festival, a sort of royal jubilee. This is held every thirty years, to celebrate the pharoah's rule and to show that he is still fit to wear the crown. Spectators from all over the country gather at the palace and cheer as the pharoah runs a special obstacle course. If he succeeds (and he always does), he is then recrowned in an elaborate ceremony. The celebrations last for weeks, and the whole country comes to a standstill. After this the pharoah tours the land in his royal barge, greeted by cheering crowds wherever he goes.

GUIDED TOURS

TEMPLE TOURS

Your tour starts in front of the high pylon gateway of the temple. Follow the crowds into the massive front courtyard, the only part of the temple open to ordinary people, and join the line waiting to consult the local god. When you reach the front, you will find yourself before a small stone carving with ears and eyes set in a wall. Ask a question, and a voice will answer from within the wall. The local people believe they are talking to the god, though you may think that the speaker is really a priest hidden in a chamber within the wall.

Once outside again, take the ferry to the west bank. On the other side, the green valley turns abruptly to desert sand. The path on the right leads to the Valley of the Kings, where the pharoahs are buried in splendid tombs. Their exact location is a secret, and access is strictly forbidden.

Be sure to visit the mortuary temple while you're here. Before entering, buy an offering from the priests at the gate. A cone-shaped loaf of bread is popular, though you may want to pay a scribe to write out a wish for you. At some temples you can even buy mummified animals, such as cats or scarab beetles, as offerings. Go through the entrance into the pillared courtyard. Do what everyone else does: Place your gift before the sacred shrine and say a quiet prayer.

Before you leave, look at the carvings on the walls. These feature hunting scenes, military victories, and the pharoah kneeling before the gods. On your way out, look at the obelisks and the huge statues of the pharoah on either side of the entrance. As the ferryman rows you back across the Nile, it's worth remembering that a large temple employs several thousand people working full time—just to keep alive the memory of one dead god-king.

GUIDED TOURS

VISITING THE PYRAMIDS

No visit to Egypt is complete without seeing the pyramids. These massive mountains of stone are on the west bank of the Nile at Giza, near the old capital city of Memphis. The pyramids are tombs built at the very dawn of Egypt's history, by the great pharoahs of the Old Kingdom (2682 to 2181 BCE).

Travel by boat to the massive temple of the pharoah Khafra to see the 23 life-size statues of the pharoah. Note the falcon god Horus, a sign of royalty, that wraps its wings around the pharoah.

From the temple, follow the sloping causeway up to the mortuary temple in the shadow of Khafra's pyramid.

On your right is the Great Sphinx, carved from a rocky outcrop 187 feet (57 meters) long and 65 feet (20 meters) high. It has the body of a crouching lion and the head of a pharoah, probably Khafra himself. The Egyptians believe that it guards his pyramid.

North of Khafra's pyramid is the Great Pyramid. The first and largest of all was built in 2550 BCE. It is huge. Each of the four sides is exactly 754 feet (230 meters) long and rises to a glittering peak 482 feet (146 meters) high. It is said to contain 2,300,000 blocks of stone, the biggest weighing ten tons each. Inside, a network of passages leads to the pharoah's burial chamber. The pyramid's sides are covered in fine limestone, polished white and gleaming in the sun. In front of it stand three smaller tombs, called the queens' pyramids because they are believed to have held the bodies of Khufu's favorite wives. Unfortunately, like all the Giza pyramids, their treasures were stolen long ago, in the period of chaos that followed the end of the Old Kingdom. How were the pyramids built? Not by slaves, but by workers who loved their pharoah and wanted to help him achieve eternal life. During the flood, when work in the fields stopped, as many as 100,000 men dragged blocks of stone up ramps to the top of the pyramid. Even with this great labor force, it took twenty years to complete Khufu's Great Pyramid.

GLOSSARY

Amun-Ra The Sun god and Egypt's most important god during the New Kingdom.

Book of the Dead More than 200 magic spells, designed to help a dead person's soul on the journey through the underworld.

Delta Flat, marshy area where a river meets the sea.

Ebony Valuable, extremely hard black wood. The Egyptians imported it from Africa.

Faience Type of glazed pottery, often blue.

Incense Substance that is burned for its pleasant smell.

Ivory Tusks and teeth of elephants, hippopotamuses, or walruses. Egyptian artists used it for carvings and furniture inlay.

Mummy Preserved body, usually wrapped in linen bandages.

Nubia Egypt's southern neighbor, an ancient land now split between Egypt and the Sudan.

Seth The evil brother of Osiris, god of death and rebirth. According to myth, Seth killed Osiris. His wife, Isis, put his body back together, to make the first mummy, and Osiris was reborn as a god.

Papyrus Reed that grew by the banks of the Nile. The Egyptians made its stems into a paper-like material to write on.

Pharaoh Egyptian king. Traditionally, the pharaoh was a man, but a woman could rule.

Pylon Massive gateway to an Egyptian temple.

Scribe Professional writer. The majority of Egyptians could not read or write, so the scribe had an important place in Egyptian society.

INDEX